How to Draw the Life and Times of
Benjamin Harrison

Melody S. Mis

The Rosen Publishing Group's
PowerKids Press™
New York

To Eva Kattau, who inspires creativity in her students and her friends

Published in 2006 by The Rosen Publishing Group, Inc.
29 East 21st Street, New York, NY 10010

First Edition

Editor: Jennifer Way
Layout Design: Ginny Chu
Photo Researcher: Martin A. Levick

Illustrations: All illustrations by Michelle Innes.
Photo Credits: Pp. 4, 7, 22 (right) © Corbis; pp. 8, 9, 10, 14 (left) Library of Congress Prints and Photographs Division; p. 12 Courtesy of Miami University; p. 14 (right) © Tria Giovan/Corbis; p. 16 Chicago Historical Society, G1920.6B; p. 18 Library of Congress Geography and Map Division; p. 20 "Cornwall Centre", Alma Place, Redruth, Cornwall (TR15 2AT) p. 22 (left) © Bettmann/Corbis; p. 24 Museum of the North American Indian, New York, USA/Bridgeman Art Library; p. 26 Picture History; p. 28 National Portrait Gallery, Smithsonian Institution/Art Resource, NY. Painting owned by and used with permission of Harrison Residence Hall, Purdue University.

Library of Congress Cataloging-in-Publication Data

Mis, Melody S.
How to draw the life and times of Benjamin Harrison / Melody S. Mis.— 1st ed.
p. cm. — (A kid's guide to drawing the presidents of the United States of America) Includes index.
ISBN 1-4042-3000-9
1. Harrison, Benjamin, 1833–1901—Juvenile literature. 2. Presidents—United States—Biography—Juvenile literature. 3. Drawing—Technique—Juvenile literature. I. Title. II. Series.
E702.M65 2006
973.8'6'092—dc22

Printed in China

Contents

Benjamin Harrison

Benjamin Harrison came from a family that had served the nation since the American Revolution. Harrison was named after his great-grandfather, Benjamin Harrison, who had signed the Declaration of Independence. Harrison's grandfather William Henry Harrison was the ninth U.S. president. His father, John Scott Harrison, was a U.S. congressman.

Benjamin Harrison was born on August 20, 1833, in North Bend, Ohio. He was the second child born to John and Elizabeth Harrison. At age 14, Harrison went to school at Farmer's College, in Cincinnati, Ohio. In 1850, Harrison enrolled in Miami University in Oxford, Ohio, graduating with honors two years later. While at Miami Harrison began courting Caroline Scott. He graduated in 1852, and married Caroline a year later.

After Harrison graduated from Miami University, he studied law for two years in Cincinnati, Ohio. In 1854, he moved to Indianapolis, Indiana, where he began practicing law. In 1862, Harrison formed the 70th Indiana Regiment to fight against the Southern army during the Civil War. This regiment served in several important battles, including the Battle of Peachtree Creek in Georgia and the Battle of Nashville in Tennessee. When the war ended in 1865, Harrison returned to Indianapolis. There he continued practicing law until 1880, when he was elected a U.S. senator. In 1888, the Republican Party nominated Harrison as their presidential candidate to run against Grover Cleveland, who was running for reelection. Harrison won the election and became the nation's twenty-third president.

You will need the following supplies to draw the life and times of Benjamin Harrison:

✓ A sketch pad   ✓ An eraser   ✓ A pencil   ✓ A ruler

These are some of the shapes and drawing terms you need to know:

Horizontal Line	——	Squiggly Line	∿
Oval	⬭	Trapezoid	⏢
Rectangle	▭	Triangle	△
Shading	▰	Vertical Line	|
Slanted Line	/	Wavy Line	∼

The Centennial President

Benjamin Harrison is called the Centennial President, because he began his presidency in 1889, 100 years after George Washington became the nation's first president. During the first two years after Harrison took office, he opened up the Oklahoma Territory for settlement and admitted six new states to the Union. These states were South Dakota, North Dakota, Washington, Montana, Wyoming, and Idaho. This was more territory than had been added under any president who had come before him.

Harrison signed a bill that established Yosemite National Park in California. Harrison also formed trade agreements with several foreign countries and settled a disagreement over the control of the Samoan Islands with Germany and Great Britain.

Harrison was nominated for a second presidential term in 1892. He did not campaign, because he was too busy taking care of his sick wife Caroline. He lost the election to Grover Cleveland, who had been president before Harrison.

Benjamin Harrison is shown here giving a speech on March 4, 1889, when he was sworn in as president. One of Harrison's accomplishments while president was organizing the Pan-American Conference, which good relations among North American and South American countries.

Benjamin Harrison's Indiana

Indiana

This is the commanding officer's quarters at Fort Harrison. The picture was taken in 1911, while the area was in use as an army training camp.

Map of the United States of America

Benjamin Harrison is the only president to have come from Indiana. Although he was born in Ohio, Harrison spent most of his adult life in Indiana. The state honored Harrison by naming the Fort Harrison State Park in Indianapolis after him. The Fort Harrison State Park began as an army training camp in 1904. For the next 90 years, the camp was used to train soldiers.

When the army camp closed in 1995, it was turned into the Fort Harrison State Park. Today Fort Harrison State Park is a favorite place for people who like to watch birds. More than 82 different types of birds make the park their summer home. The park also provides hiking trails, outdoor eating areas, a golf course, and several lakes for fishing.

After Harrison died in 1901, he was buried in a stone tomb at Crown Hill Cemetery in Indianapolis. Crown Hill is the third largest nongovernment cemetery in the United States. Visitors can take a tour of the cemetery if they want to see Harrison's tomb and learn more about the twenty-third president.

Benjamin Harrison is buried in this grave at Crown Hill Cemetery in Indianapolis, Indiana.

The Benjamin Harrison Home

Benjamin Harrison's birthplace in North Bend, Ohio, burned down in 1858. Today there is a marker where the home once stood. Fortunately, the house in Indianapolis,  where Harrison spent his final years, still exists. Harrison built this brick house, above, in 1874.

In 1888, Harrison used the long porch of his house to conduct his "front porch" campaign for the presidency. His favorite room was the library, where he met with friends and guests. He was in the library when he received the news that he had been elected president. Harrison died at his Indianapolis home on March 13, 1901.

Today the Harrison home is a museum, displaying more than 14,000 objects from Harrison's life. One of the home's most unusual objects is a wooden cane that had the heads of all the former presidents carved into it. The museum is open to the public.

1

You will be drawing the Benjamin Harrison home. To begin draw a rectangle as a guide for the house.

2

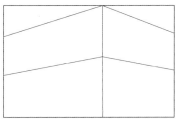

Draw a vertical line as a guide for the corner of the house. Add four slanted lines as guides for the house's two stories.

3

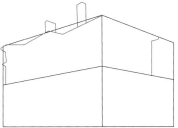

Erase the top of the guide rectangle. Next outline the shape of the roof and the sides of the house using slanted and straight lines. Add the shapes of the two chimneys.

4

Erase the guides for the top story. Use straight lines to outline the front porch. Add vertical lines for columns. Add the lines above the porch. Draw the squiggly line on the left side.

5

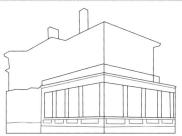

Erase extra lines. Add all the straight and slanted lines to the porch area. Draw rectangles under the porch railing. Draw the squiggly horizontal line on the left side.

6

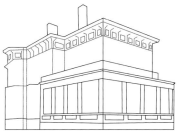

Add detail along the roof's edge using slanted lines and rectangles. Add four vertical lines on the left side of the house to show where the corners of the house are.

7

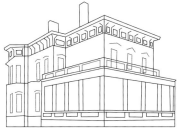

Draw the windows using rectangles and straight lines. Add shapes above the windows that look like upside-down V's. Add detail in the railing above the porch using straight lines.

8

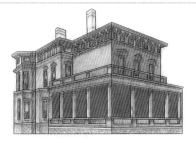

Finish by adding more detail and shading your house. Notice that the porch is very dark. Great job!

Miami University

In 1850, Harrison entered Miami University in Oxford, Ohio. He was a good student and made many friends during his two years at the university, where he studied Latin, Greek, and science. While he was at Miami University, Harrison  joined the Union Literary Society, which was a debating club. To debate means to take one side of an issue and talk about it with someone who has taken the other side of the same issue. Harrison was an excellent debater and speaker, which helped him later in his law practice and political life. He could give powerful speeches without even preparing for them.

Miami University was established in 1809, and it was named after the Miami Native Americans who once lived in the area. In the center of the grounds is the university seal, which was created in 1826. Miami University later honored Benjamin Harrison by naming a building, Harrison Hall, after him.

1

You will be drawing Miami University's seal. Begin by drawing a small circle inside a larger circle.

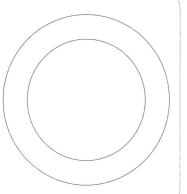

2

Next add small squares all around the inside of the smaller circle.

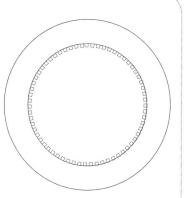

3

Erase the inner circle guide. Along the inside of the large circle, repeatedly draw the shape shown. It is a four-sided shape made with wavy lines.

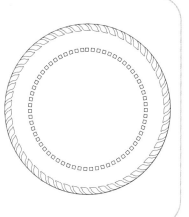

4

Write the words "SIGILLUM UNIVERSITATIS MIAMIENSIS" between the circles. Erase the large circle guide. Add a star and the two shapes as shown.

5

Draw two circles in the center. Draw the shapes inside the smallest circle. Start with a circle and a curved shape and work your way down. This will represent a globe.

6

Add two curved lines between the two circle guides. Write "PRODESSE QUAM CONSPICI." This is Latin for "to accomplish, rather than draw attention."

7

Erase the inner guide circles. Draw the shapes that represent a book and a telescope under the globe.

8

Shade the drawing to finish. Notice which shapes are the darkest. Well done!

Harrison and the Civil War

After Benjamin Harrison left Miami University, he practiced law in Indianapolis. In 1862, a year after the Civil War began, Harrison recruited men and

formed the 70th Indiana Regiment. By the end of the war, he was a brevet brigadier general. The regiment spent their first year and a half guarding railroads.

The 70th Indiana Regiment fought and won its first battle, at Peachtree Creek, Georgia, in 1864. Harrison was then sent to lead another army in the Battle of Nashville, shown above left, in Tennessee. From there Harrison went on to South Carolina to train more troops before he rejoined the 70th Regiment in April 1865, just days after the South surrendered. When Harrison went into politics, he fought to get pensions for the men who had served in the Civil War. For this he became known as the soldier's friend.

1

You will be drawing a Civil War Union general's frock coat, like the one Benjamin Harrison wore. Begin by drawing a rectangle. This will be a guide.

4

Add the lines to the shoulders and the sleeves. The shapes on the shoulders are called epaulets. Epaulets identify the rank of the person who wears the coat.

2

Using curvy lines draw the outline of the frock coat inside your rectangle. Remember to add the empty spaces between the sleeves and the body of the jacket.

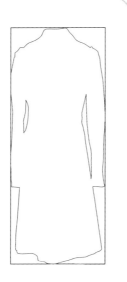

5

Draw the buttons using small, rough circles. There are 17 buttons showing. One is partly hidden under the collar. There are eight in the left column and nine in the right column. Add a line to the bottom of the right sleeve.

3

Erase the rectangle. Draw the lines on the left sleeve as shown. Add the collar and a seam down the front left of the jacket. Now add a horizontal seam where the waist of the jacket is.

6

Finish by shading the uniform. There are many folds in the fabric on the coat's arms. Folds can be created by shading some areas darker. Great job!

The Front Porch Campaign

After the Civil War ended, Benjamin Harrison returned to Indianapolis, where he practiced law. From 1881 to 1887, he served as a U.S. senator. In 1888, the Republican Party nominated Harrison as their presidential

candidate to run against President Grover Cleveland.

Harrison ran a different presidential campaign than candidates before him had done. What made his campaign different was that he stayed home and spoke to crowds from his front porch, instead of visiting other cities to make speeches. This became known as the front porch campaign. People would come to Indianapolis to hear Harrison talk. He spoke to about 300,000 people during the 80 speeches that he gave from his porch! Many of Harrison's front porch speeches were recorded in the nation's newspapers, which helped spread his ideas to people all over the country. When the election was over, Harrison had won. He became the nation's twenty-third president.

1 You will be drawing a scarf from Harrison's 1888 presidential campaign. To begin draw a square for a guide. Inside the square add three circles as shown.

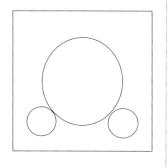

2 Next draw five rough squares inside the square you drew in step 1. Use wavy lines to draw these squares to create the look of the scarf's cloth.

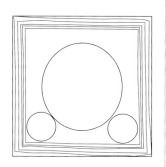

3 Erase the guide square. Draw three overlapping U.S. flags on each side of the large circle. Add flagpoles and stripes to each flag.

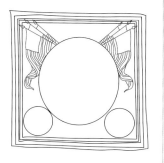

4 Using wavy lines draw the banner between the flags. Now draw small circles along the edges of all the circles you drew in step 1.

5 Erase extra lines. In the background, draw as many stars as you can fit. Leave a blank space at the top of the scarf for an eagle. Notice how some of the stars are cut off by the scarf's edge.

6 Draw the eagle on top of the banner you drew in step 4. Inside the center circle, draw the two ovals. These will be guides for the portrait of Benjamin Harrison.

7 Erase extra lines. Using the oval guides, draw Benjamin Harrison's face, clothes, body, hair, and beard.

8 Erase your oval guides. Finish with shading and detail. You can add the little house in the small circle in the lower left circle and the horse in the lower right circle. Great job!

The Oklahoma Land Run

Since 1870, Americans had been pushing the government to open the Oklahoma Territory for white settlement. Oklahoma was also known as Indian Territory, because, in the 1830s and 1840s, Native Americans had been forced to move there from the southern states.

On March 2, 1889, two days before Benjamin Harrison took office, Congress passed a law that allowed settlers into Oklahoma. On March 23, President Harrison said the Oklahoma Territory would open at noon on April 22. Shortly after his speech, people began gathering along Oklahoma's border.

By the end of the day on April 22, about 11,000 settlers had claimed land. Some were called Sooners, because they had snuck across the border at night to claim land before the official opening of the territory. Today Oklahoma's nickname is the "Sooner State." A year after the land run, Harrison signed a law that established a government in the Oklahoma Territory.

1

You will be drawing the Oklahoma Territory. Begin your drawing by making a rectangle for a guide.

2

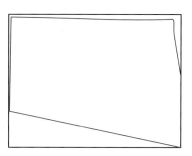

Draw Oklahoma's northern and eastern borders using slanted lines. Draw the southern and western borders using slanted lines, too. Now you have the basic shape.

3

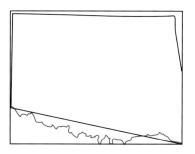

Use wavy lines to draw the southern border of the Oklahoma Territory.

4

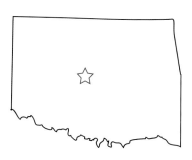

Erase the rectangular guide and the slanted line that was your guide for the southern border. Draw a star to mark Oklahoma City, which later became the state's capital.

5

Shade your drawing. You can fill in the star with a dark even tone. Nice job!

The Samoan Islands

In 1889, Benjamin Harrison avoided war with Germany and Great Britain by signing a treaty to settle a disagreement over the control of the Samoan Islands. The Samoan Islands are

located in the Pacific Ocean. They were important to the U.S. Navy, which had a refueling station there. Germany and Great Britain also wanted the islands, and they sent their warships to gain control of them. In March 1889, German, British, and American ships met at Apia, Samoa. A hurricane blew into the harbor and destroyed all but one of the ships in the harbor. This ship was Britain's HMS *Calliope*, shown above. After the hurricane harmed their ships, the three nations settled their disagreement by signing a treaty.

On June 14, 1889, Harrison signed the Berlin Treaty, which said the Samoan Islands should have an independent government. Later that year Harrison annexed Eastern Samoa for the United States.

1

You will be drawing the HMS *Calliope*. Begin by drawing a guide. Make a rectangle with a horizontal line near the bottom.

2

Draw the ship's body, or hull, using curved lines. Add two slanted lines as shown to be guides for the ship's sails.

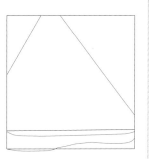

3

Erase extra lines. Add the three masts of the ship. Draw horizontal lines as guides for the sails. Add two slanted lines that meet at a point to the front of the hull.

4

Begin to draw the sails on the left side of the ship. Notice there are eight overlapping sails. Work carefully as you draw them. Add ropes as shown.

5

Erase extra lines. Using curved and slanted lines, follow the guides to add more sails to the the ship.

6

Add details to the ship's sails and masts using slanted lines and other shapes.

7

Add waves in the water using wavy lines. Use lines to indicate windows in the ship's hull. Add the two slanted lines to the side of the ship as shown.

8

To finish shade the ship. The hull is very dark. Notice how the shading in the sails makes them look curved. Add some shading to the waves in the water. Great work!

The Sherman Anti-trust Act

In 1890, Benjamin Harrison passed the Sherman Anti-trust Act. It banned monopolies, which were created when companies completely took over certain products or services. This meant that monopolies were able to charge unfairly high prices.

In the late 1800s, John D. Rockefeller, shown right, owned one of the largest monopolies, the Standard Oil Company, shown in the cartoon on the left. Rockefeller created the monopoly by buying most of the U.S. oil refineries, which turned oil into gasoline and other products. Harrison believed that monopolies hurt small businesses, because they could not compete with the large companies. Harrison wanted to protect the small businesses. That is why he passed the Sherman Anti-trust Act.

1

You will be drawing John D. Rockefeller, who owned the Standard Oil Company. Begin by drawing a rectangle. Inside the rectangle there are ovals for the head and shoulders and slanted lines for the body and arm.

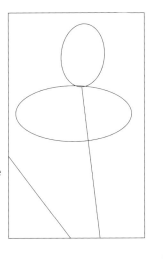

2

Using the oval guides, draw the outline of his neck, shoulders, arms, and body. Draw guides in the shape of a cross for the face.

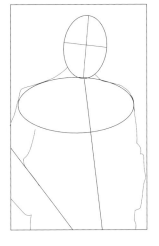

3

Erase the shoulder and arm guides. Draw the jacket and vest. Notice that the slanted line you drew in step 1 marks the middle of his body. Add the wavy line for the bottom of his vest. Draw the cuff on his left hand. His hands are in his pockets.

4

Erase the body guide. Draw the tie and shirt collar as shown. Draw the wavy line where the vest closes. Add buttons to the jacket and vest. Begin to outline the head and ears following the outside of the oval guide.

5

Erase the head oval. Use the horizontal guide to draw the eyes. Use the vertical line to draw the nose and mouth. Add the hairline and lines in the ears. Shade in the small buttons.

6

Erase the face guides and shade the drawing. The jacket is very dark and the vest has a pattern on it. Wonderful job!

The Battle of Wounded Knee

In December 1890, Benjamin Harrison sent U.S. soldiers to protect white settlers in South Dakota. The Sioux Native Americans there had been participating in a religious ceremony called the Ghost Dance. The dance was a way of protesting changes to the Sioux way of life that had been

brought about by white settlers. The Sioux believed the dance would return the world to the way things had been before settlers came. During the Ghost Dance, Sioux women would wear special dresses. The dresses had symbols on them, such as birds.

The protest scared white settlers, who wanted the government to protect them. The soldiers that Harrison sent to South Dakota fought the Sioux at Wounded Knee Creek. More than 250 Sioux, including women and children, were killed. Today historians consider the battle to be one of the most shameful events in American history.

1

You will be drawing a Ghost Dance shirt. Begin by drawing two rectangles. These will be your guides.

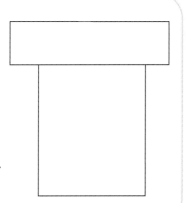

2

Inside the bottom rectangle, draw the outline of the bottom of the shirt using curved lines.

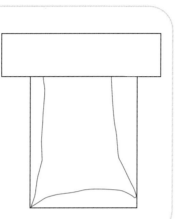

3

Erase the bottom guide rectangle. Next use the top guide to draw the sleeves and neck of the shirt.

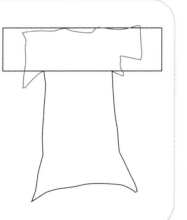

4

Erase the top guide rectangle. Using squiggly and curved lines, draw the fringes. There are fringes hanging from the bottom and sides of the shirt and sleeves.

5

Add one more row of fringe along the front of the shirt using squiggly and curved lines.

6

Draw five birds and a turtle on the shirt. The Sioux believed that birds brought messages to and from the spirit world. The turtle is believed to have brought the soil to create Earth.

7

In the remaining areas of the shirt, add stars. Follow the pattern shown here.

8

Finish the dress by shading. Keep the stars light. Great job!

Ellis Island

In 1890, Benjamin Harrison ordered the construction of a new building to  process the large number of new immigrants entering the United States. Harrison recognized the need for a large facility where immigrants could be quickly processed before they entered the country. He chose Ellis Island, in New York City's harbor to be the location for the center. It opened on January 1, 1892.

When immigrants arrived on Ellis Island, their names and countries of origin were recorded. Then they were checked for illnesses by doctors. This was done so that illnesses would not be spread in the country. Immigrants were then questioned by officials to make sure they were entering the country legally.

Between 1892 and 1954, 12 million immigrants passed through Ellis Island. They are the ancestors of more than 100 million citizens who live in America today. Ellis Island closed in 1954, and it reopened in 1990 as a museum of immigration.

1

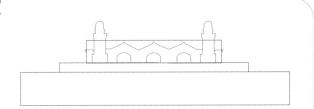

You will be drawing the building on Ellis Island. To begin draw three rectangles stacked on top of each other. These will be your guides as you draw the different levels of the building.

2

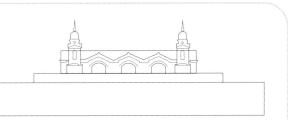

Draw the two towers. Add three windows between the towers. Draw the ledge above the windows using slanted lines. Continue the ledge to the edge of the top rectangle.

3

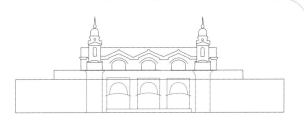

Erase extra lines. Add detail to the towers, including the pointed tops. Draw more lines above the three windows. Add the lines on the left and right sides as shown.

4

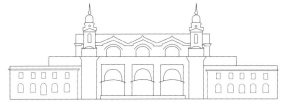

Erase extra lines. Add lines for the lower halves of the towers. Between the towers add three rectangles with arches and curved lines. Draw the shape beneath the rectangles.

5

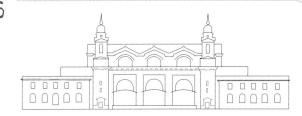

Erase extra lines. Draw 10 windows on either side of the building. Notice that some have curved tops and some are rectangles. Add a vertical line and a long, horizontal trapezoid to each side of the building.

6

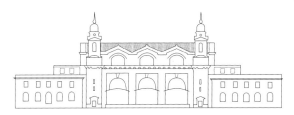

Using half circles and squiggly lines, add detail above the building's entrance. Draw small rectangles in the bottom parts of the towers. Then add lines around the bottom rectangles.

7

Add many vertical lines to the roof. Add two windows on either side of the building. Draw horizontal and vertical lines near these windows. Add a V above each entrance.

8

Shade the building to finish. Look closely at the photo to help you. Add as many details as you like. Great job!

Harrison's Legacy

In 1892, Benjamin Harrison was nominated for a second term in office. Harrison lost the election to popular former president Grover Cleveland. Just  before the election, Caroline Harrison died from an illness called tuberculosis.

After Harrison retired from office, he returned to his home and law practice in Indianapolis. In 1896, Harrison married Mary Lord Dimmick, who was Caroline's niece. They had one child. Harrison died of pneumonia at age 67 on March 13, 1901.

Many historians today accuse Harrison of not addressing the economic problems that faced the nation during his presidency. He is seen as having done better in foreign affairs because he helped the United States play a larger part in global affairs. Overall today's historians view Harrison as an average president.

1

Start your drawing of Benjamin Harrison by making the two rectangular guides.

2

Inside your guides add four oval guides. The two small ovals are guides for the hands and the two larger ovals are guides for the head and chest.

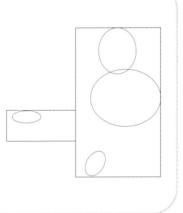

3

Draw the outline of the jacket. Notice the small line added at the neck. Draw a shape as shown as a guide for the book Harrison holds.

4

Add the pages of the book. Draw the hands inside the oval guides. Notice that his hand is partly hidden by the book. Add the cuffs of his shirt.

5

Erase the hand guides and the left rectangular guide. Draw the tie and the collar of the jacket. Add a line to make the jacket opening. Draw the desk under the book as shown.

6

Erase extra lines. Add a wavy line to the back of the jacket. Draw two lines on the face. These are guides for drawing the face. Outline the hair and beard using wavy lines.

7

Erase the oval head guide. Draw the hair and beard using wavy lines. Use the guides to help you draw the face. Add the ear.

8

Erase the face guides. Finish by shading your drawing. The jacket and tie are dark. Fantastic job!

Timeline

1833 Benjamin Harrison is born in North Bend, Ohio, on August 20.

1852 Harrison graduates from Miami University.

1853 Harrison marries Caroline "Carrie" Scott on October 20.

1854 Harrison moves to Indianapolis, Indiana, to practice law.

1862-1865 Harrison leads the 70th Indiana Regiment in the Civil War. He rises to the rank of brevet brigadier general.

1864 The 70th Regiment wins the Battle of Peachtree Creek in Georgia and the Battle of Nashville in Tennessee.

1865 Harrison returns to Indianapolis to continue his law practice.

1881-1887 Harrison serves as a U.S. senator.

1889-1893 Harrison serves as U.S. president.

1889 The Oklahoma Territory is opened for settlement.
North Dakota, South Dakota, Washington, and Montana are admitted as states.
The first Pan-American Conference is held.
The United States gains control of Eastern Samoa.

1890 Idaho and Wyoming are admitted as states.
Harrison passes the Sherman Anti-trust Act, the Sherman Silver Purchase Act, and the McKinley Tariff Act.
The Battle of Wounded Knee occurs.

1892 Caroline Harrison dies on October 25.
Harrison loses the presidential election to Grover Cleveland.

1896 Harrison marries Mary Lord Dimmick.

1901 Harrison dies on March 13.

Glossary

American Revolution (uh-MER-uh-ken reh-vuh-LOO-shun) Battles that soldiers from the colonies fought against Britain for freedom, from 1775 to 1783.

ancestors (AN-ses-turz) Relatives who lived long ago.

annexed (A-neksd) Took over or added to.

centennial (sen-TEH-nee-ul) Having to do with a hundredth anniversary.

ceremony (SER-ih-moh-nee) A special series of actions done on certain occasions.

Civil War (SIH-vul WOR) The war fought between the Northern and the Southern states of America from 1861 to 1865.

Congress (KON-gres) The part of the government that makes laws. It includes the Senate and House of Representatives.

Declaration of Independence (deh-kluh-RAY-shun UV in-duh-PEN-dints) An official announcement signed on July 4, 1776, in which American colonists stated they were free of British rule.

defend (dih-FEND) To protect.

facility (fuh-SIH-luh-tee) Something built for a certain function.

foreign (FOR-in) Outside one's own country.

immigrants (IH-muh-grunts) People who leave their country to go live in another country.

monopolies (muh-NAH-puh-leez) Businesses owned by one group.

nominated (NAH-mih-nayt-ed) Suggested that someone or something should be given an award or a position.

pensions (PEN-shunz) Money paid when people retire from a job.

pneumonia (nooh-MOHN-ya) An illness that people can get in their lungs.

recruited (ree-KROOT-ed) Signed up new soldiers for the military.

regiment (REH-jih-ment) A group in the military.

surrendered (suh-REN-durd) Gave up.

symbols (SIM-buhlz) Objects or pictures that stand for something.

tomb (TOOM) A place where a dead person is buried.

Union (YOON-yun) The United States.

Index

Web Sites

Due to the changing nature of Internet links, PowerKids Press has developed an online list of Web sites related to the subject of this book. This site is updated regularly. Please use this link to access the list:
www.powerkidslinks.com/kgdpusa/bharrison/